T0368428

AFFIRMATIONS IN MEDICINE

Little Pep Talks for Medical Students

By
David L. Taylor and Susan M. Cheng
as composed by Veda Nagubandi

Balboa Press books may be ordered through booksellers or by contacting:

Balboa Press
A Division of Hay House
1663 Liberty Drive
Bloomington, IN 47403
www.balboapress.com
844-682-1282

Photo credit for Susan Cheng Headshot: Lisa Helfert, email: lisa@lisahelfert.com, https://lisahelfert.com/

Interior Image Credit: Adaah Sayyed and Tejasvi Peesay

ISBN: 979-8-7652-4963-5 (sc)
979-8-7652-4962-8 (e)

Library of Congress Control Number: 2024902685

Print information available on the last page.

Balboa Press rev. date: 03/27/2024

BALBOA.PRESS
A DIVISION OF HAY HOUSE

A crowdsourced collection of affirmations and short stories by students, faculty, and staff at the **Georgetown University School of Medicine**

Authors' Note: Some of the affirmations in our book reference a faith tradition and are the personal perspective of the contributor. All faith traditions and other forms of affirmation are welcome and encouraged in one's personal life's journey.

DEDICATION

For my parents, Gloria & Donald Taylor;
grandparents, Rose and John Perry, Sr; and spouse, Donna Taylor:

your life's journeys are a continuing inspiration to me
and anchor the affirming wisdom I can share with others.

- David L. Taylor

For my parents, Linda & Michael Cheng,

who have made every possibility real in my life with their sacrifice,
their desire to give back to the world, and their own affirmations of resilience for me.

For my husband, Joe, for his boundless belief in me
& support to make all things good happen.

- Susan M. Cheng

ACKNOWLEDGMENTS

We would like to thank all of our Georgetown University School of Medicine students, the Georgetown Experimental Medical Studies program, and the pathway programs who contributed their anecdotes and affirmations to this book. We would also like to extend a special thank you to the alumni who returned to spread their words of wisdom to the next generation of physicians through this book.

This book would not have been possible without the efforts of our talented team - Veda Nagubandi (writer and editor), Dr.Tejasvi Peesay and Dr. Adaah Sayyed (illustrators), and Georgetown University's Director of Scholarly Publishing, Carol Sargent.

Furthermore, we would like to extend a special thanks to the individuals who contributed inspiring affirmations and anecdotes that are featured throughout this book. These individuals include - Sunny Mathaun, Goodness Odagbodo, Jai Won Jung, Yasmine White, Mariel Z. Ante, Emmanuella Akyeampong, Rotsen Rocha, Andrew Meshnick, Summer McCloud, Berline Francis, Brittney Rodriguez, Kiersten Sydnor, Pei-Ying Kobres, Francis Navarra, Jasmine Rice, Adedamola Badewa, Jason Chavez, Marsiyana Henricus, Tyrel Powell, Parsa Mahmoudi, Magdalena Macias, and Mariama Jallow-Olanrewaju.

Lastly, we are grateful for the support and contributions from our colleagues and peers at Georgetown University, team members at the Office of Diversity, Equity, Inclusion & Belonging, and Dr. Mfoniso Okon.

TABLE OF CONTENTS

MEET THE TEAM

David L. Taylor, M.Ed.

Senior Associate Dean for Student Learning

David L. Taylor joined the Georgetown University School of Medicine family in July 1990. In his role as Senior Associate Dean for Student Learning, Dean Taylor is responsible for initiatives that promote the retention and advancement of medical students through the four-year curriculum. He utilizes knowledge and skills in educational philosophy and research, student and instructor interrelationships, advising and counseling, and learning and study strategies to implement academic support services essential to students' academic success, the medical education mission and the quality of the learning experience. Dean Taylor is also the Director of the Georgetown Experimental Medical Studies (GEMS) program, which targets underrepresented and disadvantaged students aspiring to the profession of medicine. GEMS serves as a rich network of future medical students supporting Georgetown's commitment to diversity in the health professions.

Dean Taylor is the recipient of multiple awards, including the District of Columbia American College of Physicians Award for Advancing Careers of Minority Physicians (2022), the James S. Ruby Faculty Appreciation Award (2020) for exceptional service to the Georgetown University alumni community, the Mayoral Proclamation of Excellence Award (2017) for outstanding medical education programs in service to the residents of the District of Columbia, and the Georgetown University Presidential Excellence Award (2015) for exemplary service in medical student advising and support.

Dean Taylor is a graduate of Howard University and George Mason University and is married to Rev. Dr. Donna Taylor, Pastor, Andrew Chapel United Methodist Church. They are the proud parents of two adult children, Warren (Active-Duty Navy) and Whitney, and enjoy travel with their three grandchildren, Sanaa, Garfield, and Skylar.

Susan M. Cheng, Ed.L.D., MPP

Senior Associate Dean for Diversity, Equity, Inclusion and Belonging

Dr. Susan M. Cheng is the Senior Associate Dean for Diversity, Equity, Inclusion & Belonging and Associate Professor of Family Medicine at Georgetown University School of Medicine. In her role, she prioritizes systemic efforts to address structural inequities at the school including academic preparation, inclusive learning environments, curricular reform, and faculty development with a focus on anti-racism/anti-oppression. She was formerly part of the founding team of Beyond Z (now Braven), an early-stage college to career start-up focused on accelerating diverse talent, where she directed college curriculum and program design for low-income, first-generation college students. Before joining this venture, Dr. Cheng was an Associate Partner at NewSchools Venture Fund where she focused on human capital investment and management assistance for the firm's teacher preparation portfolio ventures in the Learning to Teach Fund. While at NewSchools, Dr. Cheng co-launched design teams focused on collaborating on solutions to address cross-sector challenges impacting teacher preparation. Prior to NewSchools, she joined Chancellor Michelle Rhee's transition team for the District of Columbia Public Schools (DCPS). While with DCPS, she focused on human capital recruitment and talent development, organizational culture building, and designing and implementing a performance-management system for the central office.

Dr. Cheng also created and ran the Urban Education Leaders Internship Program (UELIP) and launched the Teachers Central to Leadership (TCTL) central office fellowship for DCPS teachers. Prior to DCPS, she volunteered with Partners in Health in Rwanda, worked in the DC Mayor's office, and managed a portfolio of education diversity and environmental justice programs for the Greenlining Institute in California.

Dr. Cheng graduated summa cum laude from UCLA with a Bachelor of Arts in communications and a minor in education. She has a Master's in Public Policy from the Harvard Kennedy School and a Doctor in Education Leadership (Ed.L.D.) from the Harvard Graduate School of Education. While at the Kennedy School, Susan co-designed the Community Building workshop to promote campus diversity and helped to form the ALANA (African, Latino(a), Asian, and Native American) Group Chapter on campus. During her doctoral studies, she was a Freshman Proctor for Massachusetts Hall at Harvard College, supporting the academic and social development of 28 first year students.

Dr. Cheng is a proud resident of Ward 5, and lives in the Eckington neighborhood of Washington, D.C., with her husband, Joe and their three children, Zadie, Finn, Poppy and their pup, Taro.

Veda Nagubandi, BS

Veda Nagubandi is a graduate of Georgetown University's School of Foreign Service where she majored in Science, Technology, and International Affairs and concentrated on biotechnology and global health. While at Georgetown, she was also an Innovation Associate for the Office of Diversity, Equity, Inclusion & Belonging (ODEIB) where she worked closely under Dean Cheng's mentorship. Currently, she is working on health disparities research initiatives that promote dermatology health equity at the University of Pennsylvania.

Adaah Sayyed, MD

Adaah Sayyed is a PGY-1 Plastic and Reconstructive Surgery resident at Southern Illinois University. She hopes to use her artistic expertise to help achieve both form and function for her patients through plastic surgery. She recently graduated from Georgetown University School of Medicine where she completed the Population Health Scholar Track, learning how to integrate a public health and health policy lens into her clinical career. She also took part in nonprofit work with organizations such as Medical Supply Drive and Physicians for Human Rights. She is passionate about research and hopes to address health inequities within plastic surgery in future studies. Throughout her medical career, Adaah has intertwined her passion for the arts with medicine, creating anatomic illustrations for research studies, working as a book illustrator for the Office of Diversity, Equity, Inclusion & Belonging, and creating graphic designs for medical clubs and organizations.

Tejasvi Peesay, MD

Tejasvi Peesay is a categorical Internal Medicine resident at the McGaw Medical Center of Northwestern University. She graduated with a Bachelor of Science from the University of Maryland, College Park (2017) and from Georgetown University School of Medicine with a Doctor of Medicine (2022). At Georgetown, she was involved in several service initiatives and founded a nonprofit during the pandemic, called Medical Supply Drive. She served on the board of Arts and Medicine and was co-president of Healing through the Arts. Tejasvi's watercolor piece landed on the cover of Georgetown's arts magazine. Her efforts culminated in receiving the Stephen Ray and Ellen Mitchell Leadership Award and serving as Vice President of the Gold Humanism Honor Society. At Northwestern, she is in the Women's Health Track and is passionate about quality improvement projects and advocating for underrepresented populations. She hopes to pursue a career in cardiology.

INTRODUCTION

Build and Belong

Students, especially those who are underrepresented in medicine, can experience a lack of belonging and a sense of social disconnection during their path to physicianship. As a way to address this issue, we utilized evidence-based strategies to cultivate the Build & Belong initiative at Georgetown University School of Medicine.

The Build & Belong initiative[1] was a peer-to-peer support program that included self-reflections, affirming video messages, discussion sessions, and future letters to peers. The initiative was a big hit among students, as it helped reduce feelings of social isolation while increasing feelings of mindfulness, trust, assurance, connectedness, and belonging.

Studies indicate that medical students and residents often face burnout and emotional distress due to experiencing a lack of support. Risks for these adverse outcomes decrease among medical students who have increased support. This book is a personification of the Build & Belong initiative to uplift students by increasing their sense of support (McLuckie, 2018). We hope that our book serves as a guide for students of all backgrounds to navigate the challenges of medical school, helping build shared resiliency among students on the medical school journey and normalize doubts about feelings of belonging in medical school.

As you read through the book, you will find a series of affirmations and short anecdotes. We hope that each affirmation and story contribute to your support network by providing examples of shared struggles and the growth that resulted from them. Stories of recovering from missteps shared with you can help fill up your resiliency reservoir and defeat the challenges that may arise on your path of professional identity formation in medicine.

Ultimately, medicine is a career filled with promises of a culture of teamwork and cooperative learning. In an effort to engage learners through authentic affirmations, we curated this book of anecdotes and assurances from students, alumni, and colleagues to help create the spark of self-belief in you that will help you reach your life's calling. We hope you enjoy reading our book as much as we enjoyed creating it, and we hope that you find the support and inspiration necessary on your journey to physicianship through the affirmations, anecdotes, and assurances provided. Welcome to your very own peer support network that you can revisit any time you need or want as you navigate your journey into medicine!

---

[1] Cheng SM, Taylor DL, Fitzgerald AA, Kuo CC, Graves KD. Build & Belong: A Peer-Based Intervention to Reduce Medical Student Social Isolation. Teach Learn Med. 2022 Oct-Dec;34(5):504-513. doi: 10.1080/10401334.2021.1984921. Epub 2021 Nov 11. PMID: 34763586; PMCID: PMC9091060.

SECTION 1:

Purpose

Research shows that intrinsic motivation, which is one's inherent drive to work towards and achieve a goal, is critical to succeeding academically and continuing with your medical education. Not only is there evidence for the benefits of high intrinsic motivation towards medical education achievement, but there is also strong evidence that individuals with low controlled motivation – which is incentives derived from external regulation such as a desire for rewards or fear of punishment – have higher success in their medical education journey.[2]

This evidence suggests that your internal drive, your purpose, and your Why for pursuing medicine are the critical factors towards achieving your goals and staying on track.

The following chapters explore your sense of purpose, expand on why it is important, and how to sustain your purpose in the presence of challenges.

---

[2] Wouters, A., Croiset, G., Galindo-Garre, F. et al. Motivation of medical students: selection by motivation or motivation by selection. BMC Med Educ 16, 37 (2016). https://doi.org/10.1186/s12909-016-0560-1

SECTION 1 OPENING:

Dean Taylor's Letter

Learning for Life's Calling:
Success as the Other Side of Failure

There were four formative figures in my life: Gloria Taylor, Oscar Nims, Joy Williams, and Arthur Hoyte. After having lost my father at a young age, my mother, Gloria, was my biggest supporter. She often stated that I could be anything that I wanted to become, even the president of the United States. Not only did her constant affirmations instill a sense of confidence in me, but her desire to foster my intellectual development sparked my interest in medicine. As I acted on this interest, I faced many challenges, but having supportive faculty was crucial in helping me face these challenges. This brings me to the second formative figure: Oscar.

Dr. Oscar Nims, my mentor during my undergraduate years, said "As a medical student, you may wake up one day and feel unsettled, like your entire body is shaking at that moment. You're going to question yourself and ask, do I really want to pursue medicine? And in that moment, you should know that it's going to be ok." As I pursued my medical degree at Howard University College of Medicine, one day, I woke up feeling eerily like the way that Oscar had described. I ran to the school's psychiatrist's office and felt the door reverberate as I knocked once, knocked twice, and finally knocked for the third time.

Dr. Duckett, the school psychiatrist, had previously pointed out that he was in a session with a student if his door was closed. On my third knock, Dr. Duckett peered out and made my fears come true, he was preoccupied.

What should I do now?

I went back to my apartment to reevaluate my journey. While I was navigating the intense coursework of medical school and trying to keep my head above water through the overwhelming feelings of intensity, this moment of reflection provided a moment of reprieve. My mother's and Oscar's words helped me sit down and evaluate my current state. Their words reminded me to stay motivated and provided me with the effective discipline necessary to reflect on my future with intentionality. I met with the Dean of Students and took a leave of absence.

The opportunity to freely explore other career options in medical education provided me with affirming insight into the possible professional aspirations outside of a medical school path.

Now, my story may seem like a failure with respect to achieving the goal of becoming a physician, given the deviation from the structured path to medical school that each of you are on.

However, this challenge actually opened the door to my future success in medical education and how I might use my gifts and talents to help students achieve their calling to the profession of medicine.

It equipped me with the resilience necessary to own my destiny and navigate life's challenges.

It takes bravery to understand who you are and your true purpose in serving others.

My story's third and fourth formative figures are Dean Joy Williams and Dr. Arthur Hoyte, who mentored me in medical education and student development and supported my professional path to help students "learn how to learn" in medicine. Arthur and Joy saw my potential to pass on the life lessons I had learned in my brief medical school journey, as well as my unique gifts and passion for advising and teaching effective learning strategies for the journey

in medicine. I started mentoring students from that point onwards, which blossomed into a 33-year career at Georgetown, the results of which would be best summed up by the words of my Pastor who said: "God did not call you to be the king. He called you to be the kingmaker and the queenmaker. You thought you were called to be the king's physician, but he called you with all your gifts and talents to help train king and queen physicians who would heal the land. Do you see the powerful responsibility in that call? Do you accept your calling?"

During my years as a mentor, advisor, and educator at Georgetown University, these are the lessons that I share with my students: continually reflect on your successes and challenges as you journey through your life's calling for the profession of medicine. There will be inevitable, short moments of failure on your ultimate successful path to your purpose of service as a physician. Fully embrace these moments with the support of mentors – we can learn that it is ok to have moments of disappointment, as these moments help us learn effective ways to deal with our fears of failure; in doing so, we will learn with confidence that success is truly the other side of failure. Through this book of affirmations, Susan and I hope to instill this lesson through examples of shared experiences that can help you stay the course and achieve success in your calling to service through the profession of medicine.

CHAPTER 1

Why Why Why:
What is Your Why in Learning?

Ever since our journey within the educational system began, we are constantly exposed to the notion that learning is a one-dimensional process. We are expected to learn the facts presented to us, regurgitate this information on standardized tests, and (maybe) utilize these facts in our future careers. However, in order to even begin to understand the abstract enigma called *learning truly,* one must first shift the paradigm and view learning more so as a multi-dimensional process especially as it relates to medicine.

The belief that there is only one dimension to medical learning is most likely due to the fact that when one is trying to develop their academic skill competencies, there is a heavy emphasis placed upon memorizing pathophysiological facts. Despite this belief, medical learning is not as simple as memorizing factual information and is instead a more complex, multi-dimensional process. During the realization of one's medical calling, the aforementioned dimension of the medical learning process - biomedical science knowledge acquisition - is coupled with a more implicit dimension - wisdom. Here, wisdom is the ability to discern how to use knowledge to achieve meaningful patient outcomes. This second dimension of the multi-dimensional medical learning process must involve a Why.

The Why is one's motivation that pushes them to move beyond learning just for the sake of acquiring knowledge towards learning to develop the necessary skills to improve patient outcomes. Or, put more simply, moving beyond a focus on book smarts to using book smarts to build street smarts.

Establishing a strong knowledge base is a solid start toward becoming a well-rounded physician. However, it must be followed up by the development of softer skills such as effective communication, which is often required to mitigate patient suffering, and advocacy skills, which assist one in making ethical decisions that further social justice. The ability to learn these skills is oftentimes influenced by one's knowledge, meaning that it is imperative to broaden one's knowledge base continuously. However, the disposition to apply knowledge when learning essential skills in service of patients is even more vital to physician development given that medicine involves rapid knowledge turnover and continuous innovations.

As one navigates the medical learning process and attempts to discover the Why that drives them toward medicine, there are inevitable challenges that occur along the way. For instance, one may question their Why as it relates to book knowledge if they struggle with an anatomy class. Or one may question their Why as it relates to cultural humility if they witness their higher-ups disparaging patients. One may even question their ability to become a servant leader in medicine when it appears that the system is designed in a manner to limit patient care times for the sake of bolstering profits. Even in recent times, we ourselves have faced these situations with our research project, Build and Belong, receiving multiple manuscript rejections over the course of 2 years. Such setbacks can lead to self-doubt and make us our own mental saboteur.

Combating the mental saboteur requires affirmations. Mentor-provided affirmations can help you find your Why and move into your purpose by showing that embracing incompetence and holding ourselves accountable can allow us to realize that every misstep is an opportunity for growth.

Using affirming ideas to develop your Why in learning requires difficult reflection, but the more that you are honest with yourself, the more you understand that success involves utilizing your Why to work through the multi-dimensional learning process and its inevitable challenges. For us, this process involved internalizing the affirming words of our colleague and publishing mentor, Dr. Kristi Graves, Associate Dean for Faculty Development at the Georgetown University Medical Center, who ultimately helped us learn from our failed manuscript attempts to improve our workflow and finally achieve publication in 2021.

Through the process of intentional sharing and reflection, we can instill in the next generation that we are not perfect outcomes of medicine, but instead resilient works of progress trying to gain wisdom within the context of continuously evolving medical learning.

Such is the cycle of learning: taking what you learned to affirm others when helping them find their Why. This is the goal of our affirmations in medicine: to further the cycle of medical learning through reflection and celebrating missteps as the other side of success.

My "Why" for medicine is a combination of lived and learned experiences that I've had throughout my life, starting at a very young age, which gave me my childhood dream of becoming a physician. My lived experiences compose of being a caretaker for my father from the age of 8 until he succumbed to his battle with cancer when I was 11 years old. Growing up in a single parent household and experiencing dark times, especially with the healthcare system, gives me the passion to become a great physician one day.

My learned experiences compose of my time clinically volunteering at the Hospice and being able to make a direct impact on the patients who are towards the end of their lives, shadowing physicians in hospitals and learning about what physicians experience on a daily basis, serving the medically under-served population with our organization I started at school and volunteering at a medical clinic that focuses on the under-served population, the CORE program at GUSOM, and much more.

My activities, via learned experiences, have reaffirmed my obsessive passion for medicine that was initiated by lived experiences early in my life. A passion for medicine that was realized when I was taking care of my father, as a little boy, with financial instability and limited access to the benefits of quality healthcare. My "Why" is to create equal access to quality healthcare so I can save more lives as a future physician/surgeon without patients, and their families, having to deal with lack of access to quality healthcare, as every human being deserves, especially in the United States. My calling in life for medicine is not an option but a necessity.

- Sunny Mathaun

Pre-Medical Student

I like to help people. Simple, yet so valuable. Helping people is one of those things that can change your life, change your career. Helping others is not just a job, it's a lifestyle; a lifestyle that changes the world.

- Goodness Odagbodo

Pre-Medical Student

CHAPTER 2

Down and (Not) Out?
Navigating Inevitable Challenges

We've all had those moments in life that feel like we're getting sucker punched. Whether it's getting a bad grade on a midterm that you studied hard for or whether it's not getting into your dream research program, failing to achieve something important to you is always a hard knockdown. In these initial moments, right after discovering this dreadful news about a shortcoming, it can feel like you were dealt a heavy blow. However, this moment is merely temporary. Slowly, in our journey towards getting back on our feet, we begin to question how we got here in the first place.

"How did that happen? What went wrong? Did I give my best effort?" As we begin to ask & answer these questions, a shift happens.

While it's not an instantaneous recovery, analyzing our situation improves our state as we move from lying on our backs, dazed and confused, to sitting up. Through this process of questioning ourselves and seeking answers to these questions, we begin to recover from our initial failings and gain insight on how to use this to better ourselves.

However, this is not the end of our recovery process, not yet at least. Although we have made great progress so far, and it's no small feat to reach this point, our biggest hurdle is yet to come. We still need to stand up. This stage, the stage of declaring to yourself and to the world that you still have more to do, more things to learn, and more challenges to overcome, is the most important.

Here, we experience our biggest turning point as we assess our readiness for growth.

Was the self-exploration we performed during the sitting stage regarding missteps and potential solutions enough to prepare us for the next challenge? In other words, did we grow enough from our shortcomings so as not to get knocked down again by a similar challenge?

Transitioning between each stage of the recovery process - lying on our backs from the blow of the initial knockdown, sitting up as we assess the situation, and ultimately standing up to take on the next challenge – represents an important growth point. Moving from each stage as we recover from failure can help us prepare for the inevitable challenges that will present themselves as our reflection at each point acts as a springboard for the future.

Each knockdown, while always painful, is not without purpose as it plays a pivotal part in your journey by giving you a chance to train yourself to recover more quickly and see how much you have grown from the previous knockdown.

Medicine, as a field, has a particularly curious way of clouding your journey, forcing you to have tunnel vision regarding the present and concerns about what will happen in the future. What we fail to consider during these moments is our past. During each little knockdown on this difficult journey to physicianship, embracing the lessons learned from your past failures can help you refocus, reframe the situation, and prepare yourself with the strategies necessary to counteract the next challenge.

Ultimately, what exactly allows us to bounce back from being knocked down, lying on our backs, to sitting up as we regain some of our composure?

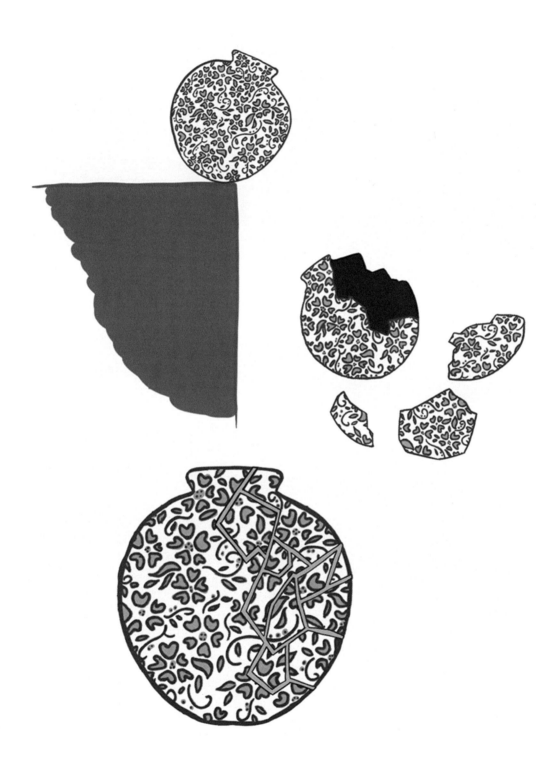

Just like a boxing coach lends his hand to his sure-spirited boxer, the initial transition is facilitated by the human spirit's resiliency and the leverage of affirmations provided by a mentor, parent, peer, or other figure. If we can't make this initial transition from the supine state to the sitting state, we need to seek out help in the form of additional affirmations that remind us of our capacity for success.

Not only can these lessons apply to medicine, but they can apply to more personal aspects of our lives as well. For instance, as a parent of three beautiful children who had to face a difficult journey towards parenthood through IVF, Susan has first-hand experience with growth points and their potential to equip us with the life lessons needed to take on the next challenge. Having difficulty fulfilling the ideal vision she had around becoming a parent on her own without medical intervention felt like a gut punch. As she was knocked down, she slowly began to sit back up, asking herself the questions and finding the answers necessary to recover from the situation.

After multiple fertility consults, affirmations that she wrote on her mirror, and encouraging words from doctors and nurses regarding potential options, she ultimately became a parent. Reflecting on the initial letdown helped her learn from the pain, which was due to her anchoring onto a certain version of her dream. This reflection allowed her to embrace a more flexible mindset, preparing her for future challenges.

In a similar fashion, you too can acknowledge growth points to overcome the next challenge.

I have gone through many failures throughout my journey. Even though my dream was to get into medical school from the beginning, I got modest undergraduate grades and MCAT scores. On top of that I was undocumented and financially unstable. I had to find a way to obtain my citizenship and get into medical school.

As a first-generation immigrant, I was stubborn. I did not ask for help and I did not know how to ask for help.

One thing that I learned from my experience is that you need to know when to ask for help. After multiple rejections from medical schools, I applied for the GEMS program. That is where I learned how and when to ask for help. This has been a vital skill that I still use to this day as a 4th year medical student and I would have not been able to come this far without this skill.

- Jai Won Jung, MD

Please make sure to always keep your mental health in mind. Medicine is a marathon not a sprint, so there will be many times where it feels overwhelming. You have already made it this far, keep going!

- Yasmine White

Medical Student

CHAPTER 3

The Sh*t Storm:
Time to Wipe and Clean Up

Boom! That's all you hear as you see a lightning bolt flash across the sky. Before you know it, you're caught in the Sh*t Storm. Maybe this Storm is a month of financial difficulties or maybe it involves a hefty workload on a tight deadline. Maybe you had foreseen the Storm coming and were able to find yourself shelter, or maybe you were caught wholly unprepared. The path to physicianship is no different. There are Storms that many have encountered during their travels along this road, and due to the difficult nature of this path, the severity of these Storms is more often than not amplified. Because of this severity, it is imperative that you know how to properly weather these Storms by building and maintaining your shield.

Some of the Storms that medical students may face along their path to physicianship typically relate to finances, housing, food, health, and/or interpersonal relations. Oftentimes, when a student is weathering a sustained Storm in one (or more) of the aforementioned categories, their mind may quickly fill with worries about surviving their medical journey. These worries, while not particularly as rare as one would hope, may preclude a foreboding outcome. However, there are plenty of actionable turning points that one can take before one reaches this state of panic, which will be discussed later.

17

There are many students in medical school who are not financially secure. Some students may be able to mitigate this via financial assistance. However, in many cases, this avenue doesn't completely resolve the issue. Because sometimes the student is not just the student, but also a sister, a brother, a parent, and a source of income for others. If the student has dependents and is responsible for the well-being of not just themselves but their family as well, the loan that was intended to assist with academic expenses becomes the loan responsible for academic, housing, food, medical expenses, etc. These socio-economic struggles may only be half the battle. There are, of course, other struggles that the student may be facing, such as relationship tensions or forms of mental hardship like depression or eating disorders.

All of these can be truly destabilizing and have the potential to threaten one's very identity; unfortunately, this is all too common in medical school. Even if the student is able to cover up their troubles for a period of time, eventually, things implode. At this point, students may present with concerning indicators such as absenteeism or greatly diminished academic performance. Sometimes, it's all too easy to get caught in a loop wherein the student struggles to navigate a hardship that only exacerbates other hardships.

How does one exit this loop?

Since navigating these Storms is not just a matter of the student's determination in medicine, but instead a concern of "Do you have the stability and the basic requirements you need to be safe to focus on your studies?," students and their institutions must collaborate on building additional support networks such that students have a lattice of reinforcements when the Storm hits.

Sometimes, this additional support network may come from a student confiding in a mentor or faculty member they trust. There may also be a proactive, experienced mentor who brings the student in for a safe, confidential discussion. Whether initiated by the student or mentor, reasonably leveraging university resources can be a valuable mitigating solution.

Take the previous discussion of students facing financial hardships. One of the things we, as deans, do is identify appropriate support options through our Office of Admissions & Financial Planning. In these times, we need to ensure that someone is there for the student. Because this process involves navigating the network of university resources on behalf of students, a collaborative effort among staff and students is required.

Another pillar of the support network comes from affirming anecdotes that can help students cope and be more present. Hearing stories from others about their struggles and solutions can be very important in crafting a stabilizing force when it may not be readily present.

Faculty mentors can be valuable sources of affirming words. As deans, we understand that opening up to our students and showing them that struggles are normal and natural is especially important. For example, Susan has discussed her challenges with infertility and challenges with getting into higher academia with her students. The pertinence of showing even senior faculty can struggle with realizing their full potential should not be understated. It can be very humanizing. And this humanity can be very inspiring because it's good to avoid the "perfect hero" archetype who has got it all figured out already and can flawlessly navigate through the system and overcome every obstacle with ease.

Despite collaborating with institutional support or adopting a positive mindset through exposure to affirming presences, sometimes students may continue to be at the mercy of the Storm.

If the Storm persists for too long without decelerating, then other alternatives, such as a leave of absence, may be required in order to minimize the combined stress of external challenges and inherent challenges associated with navigating medical school.

Regardless of the outcome of the Storm, it is important to note how you or your institution began to establish support networks and whom you began to trust during this challenging time. Keeping in touch with these individuals who assisted you in your time(s) of need can help bolster the support systems you are already establishing.

This must be done as an intentional and continual process and as a part of one's own professional development because there will always be new Storms for which one has to stay prepared. Always remember that even if you hit rock bottom, you can rebuild with the help of others. You just might need to take the first step of reaching out and trying to make a connection. If you can do this, you have the ability to build a network that can help you weather any Storm!

Losing my mom was my biggest life challenge. Amidst all the energy needed to focus in succeeding medical school, I still grieve with my family.

The hows and whys of losing her are questions that will unfortunately remain unanswered. When we are going through hardships, especially losing someone we love, there is no clarity and there is no motivation for anything. There will be self-doubt and loneliness in the process. There will be waves of tears and happiness and sometimes, you will have moments of acceptance that such hardship will never fully go away.

Knowing this, my advice to keep going is to give yourself time to heal. Reach out to your loved ones who can understand you. Recognize your emotions and speak to someone who can support you, redirect your path, if not help you learn how to push forward. More importantly, invest in your own self-care whatever that may mean to you and do not ever give up in trying to be okay while you are pursuing your dream. You are strong and capable of overcoming obstacles that will come your way. Truly, the one thing that has kept me going was my mother who imparted in me words of strength:

"No matter what happens, go go go!".

And here I am; I'm going.

- Mariel Z. Ante

Medical Student

Being a physician is a calling. It might not be everyone's destination due to the different places you'll be called to serve but it's all perspective.

Yes, the med school process/med school is hard, but so is life and you have to see the rainbow somewhere in the storm. You can do all things when you put your mind to it, seek for help when you need it, and labor for it. Many have been in your shoes, and many have made it out. I am on my way, and I will see you at the top because we are capable.

- Emmanuella Akyeampong

Pre-Medical Student

SECTION 2:

Believing

Affirmations and the resulting feelings of self-worth have evidence-based positive effects. For instance, a study regarding achievement gaps between underrepresented students and their white counterparts in STEM (science, technology, engineering and math classes) revealed that the introduction of affirmations reduced the achievement gap by mitigating the psychological and emotional aspects of stereotype threat, which is the risk of substantiating negative stereotypes about one's racial, ethnic or gender group that can often lead to low academic achievement.[3]

Our book is based on this principle to increase feelings of self-worth, self-motivation, and self-confidence through affirmations and assurances for students who need it most.

The following chapters explore the importance of affirmations in silencing those who try to bring you down, in building your peer and academic support network, and in becoming a forever dreamer who always strives to grow.

---

[3] Jordt H, Eddy SL, Brazil R, Lau I, Mann C, Brownell SE, King K, Freeman S. Values Affirmation Intervention Reduces Achievement Gap between Underrepresented Minority and White Students in Introductory Biology Classes. CBE Life Sci Educ. 2017 Fall;16(3):ar41. doi: 10.1187/cbe.16-12-0351. PMID: 28710060; PMCID: PMC5589421.

SECTION 2 OPENING:

Dean Cheng's Letter

Antidotes to the Challenges from Reaching Your Calling

I knew I always wanted to be a dean and enter higher education. However, I had a very difficult time entering the realm of higher education. My self-doubts started during my enrollment in a doctoral program at Harvard University. Nearing graduation, two deans asked me what I wanted to do with my degree during an important advising session. My reply was earnest and sincere: "Go into higher administration and be a dean!" But their response was far from encouraging.

One of the deans present proceeded to laugh in my face, saying that I needed to be more practical and that was not what the degree was intended for. At that moment, I experienced incredible pain. I had openly shared my dream with these experienced individuals, but could I stop them from hurting my dream? As my friends described me with positive adjectives like "brilliant" for graduating with my degree, these words felt hollow. These words were hard for me to believe after the searing ridicule that my dreams faced on that day. Sometimes it was difficult to go back to that memory with these advisors and shake off the sounds of their laughter and images of their smiles of disbelief on their faces.

In the face of this challenging time, I tried to rebuild myself. This process involved a lot of reflection, prayer, and experience working in the kindergarten through 12th grade space. But the most important lifeline that I had throughout all of this was my belief in myself.

A good friend of mine, Jenny, sent me a quote that follows me to today - both as my phone's screensaver and as a wall decal in my office at Georgetown School of Medicine's Office of Diversity, Equity, Inclusion & Belonging. The quote is one by E.E. Cummings that reads,

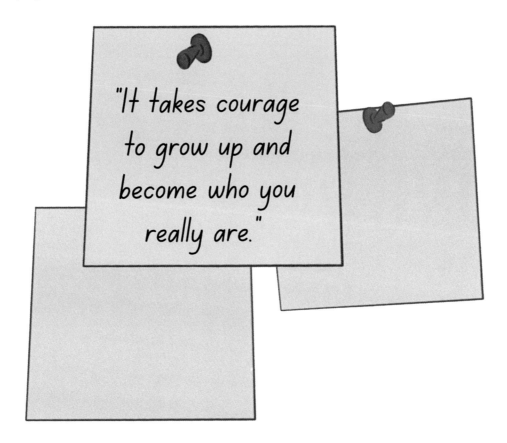

I looked at this quote every day for years as I opened my phone or read through the post-its plastered on my walls filled with encouraging self-affirmations that I had written to myself as I started receiving rejections.

No one seemed to believe that I had the courage to realize my true calling of becoming an academic dean.

As I sifted through rejection after rejection, reading this quote and other affirmations when no one around me accepted my dreams, even myself at points, helped me believe in myself.

When I didn't know I could achieve my dream, I needed to see it through like the quote said.

When I was going through times in which I was too scared to share my dream with others due to the pain that I had experienced, these positive words helped create a spark of self-belief inside of me.

Never underestimate the potential of this spark, especially since its power is too large to go unnoticed!

When I got to Georgetown University School of Medicine, Dean Joy Williams, my predecessor, told me that she was hiring for my current position. She asked me typical interview questions like "How do you know you could do this job?" but the most important question in our exchange was, "What if you don't get this job?" I will never forget that moment. With such a large degree of conviction, I exclaimed that whether it's Georgetown or not, I will be a dean in higher education! Her expression instantly changed, like when one has a stark moment of realization. At that point, I knew that she saw the spark inside of me. She knew that what I had said was going to happen. This culminated in the realization of my calling - I became an academic dean at Georgetown University School of Medicine, a career that has lasted for nearly nine years.

Without those affirmations from my friends, the quotes that I read, and my belief in myself, my newly unlocked confidence that allowed me to rebound from the incident that occurred at the beginning of my blossoming career would not have been present. I needed this confidence. I needed this courage to take that leap of faith and continue to pursue a career in higher education since higher education is what I'm meant to do with my life.

In times when you believe in your life's calling, but no one else seems to believe in your dreams, affirmations can become a lifeline. At the end of the day, you bear witness to your own dreams and these meaningful, authentic affirmations are your witnesses along the way. They represent formative figures or words that can act as antidotes to the challenges that try to poison your journey towards reaching your life's calling. And they are the life raft that can help you follow through with your commitments, even when you cannot trust others with your dreams.

The journey to medicine is very long and complicated. Without these affirmations, having the discipline to focus your intentionality becomes very challenging. For this very reason, Dave and I have curated this book of affirmations from students, alumni, and colleagues to help create the spark of self-belief in you that helped me focus on achieving my life's calling.

Susan M. Cheng

CHAPTER 4

Squash the Saboteurs Outside:
Silencing Haters

Words of haters, doubters, and naysayers tend to stick with us. For instance, when Susan was in elementary school, a fellow student told her, "You work very hard, but you aren't very smart." This painful string of words in childhood turned into a nagging voice that lingered in the back of her mind from time to time and crept behind her as a saboteur. It followed her throughout the years as she returned to this sentiment in her academic life, most especially during times she struggled and encountered a setback when she was trying to publish or conduct research. In such instances, a hater's words can be like a raggedy winter coat. The coat you outgrew, the one you may have never liked, and the one you never even asked for the day that it was unwarrantedly handed down to you. The one you feel obligated to wear when you don't. But, out of habit, it sits there in your closet.

Despite all of your reservations about the coat, you may find yourself forcing that coat onto yourself. In other words, even though the words may have been said in jest, you start to carry their burden over the years, constantly referring back to these negative comments.

How do you stop carrying around this jacket that doesn't fit and defining yourself by these hater's words?

In your medical journey, in addition to haters, there may also be doubters and naysayers. What is the difference, you may be wondering? The hater aims to knock down your success due to their own lack of direction. Haters' desires to cut others' celebrations short come from people in their own lives failing to celebrate them and their successes. Conversely, the doubter tends to sow seeds of doubt in you about your life goals. Unlike the hater, the doubter has experienced successes that have been celebrated by those around them, but the doubter has also experienced some setbacks along the way. As a result of these setbacks and a lack of affirming individuals around them, the doubter begins to doubt their ability to move forward with their goals and starts to apply this same doubtful mindset to your goals.

Similarly, a naysayer can be characterized by their constant tendency to refute the possibility of you realizing your goals. In other words, the naysayer is an advanced doubter. The selfish naysayer's desire to bring you down arises from the large range of challenges they faced throughout their life. These challenges, coupled with their lack of resilience or affirmation, cause them to hold the perspective that everything will go awry not just for them, but for you as well.

By operationalizing the differences between the negative voices that you may face on your path to physicianship, we can come to one realization.

Haters, naysayers, and doubters derive their discouraging words and actions from deep-rooted behavioral anchors caused by their desire to escape their shortcomings. To prevent these figures from deterring your path to success, you must face them head-on in the arena like a Roman gladiator. You have two solutions at hand: block them from coming into your side of the arena, or if they have already penetrated your defenses and entered your headspace, choose to ignore them via an approach that we call "intentional inoculation."

Intentional inoculation involves the adoption of a growth mindset, understanding that you and your abilities are not fixed in time and that you are ever evolving.[4] Reminding yourself of where you are now and asking yourself, "Am I the same person that I was a month ago?" is a simple way to remove yourself from a fixed, limiting mindset. Only then can you begin to realize your ability to transform your goals into reality during your journey in spite of outside voices. Adopting this mindset gives you a sense of possibility and you can be better prepared to thwart the words of the doubters, haters, and naysayers around you. Now you are more likely to shake off discouraging words that aim to stagnate your growth and get the support that you need during that point in your life. Time to stop wriggling yourself into that old jacket that should be thrown away!

Adopting a learner's mindset can be very challenging since humans tend to revert to the familiar. To ease the transition, learning something new every day, no matter how small can help keep you on your feet and take you out of your comfort zone. For instance, Susan started to take up the hobby of bouldering at a local climbing gym last year, even though she is afraid of heights. This new skill, as challenging as it is, is mentally stimulating and keeps her ready to acknowledge her growth so that she isn't bogged down by outside voices.

In addition to adopting the growth mindset, surrounding yourself with your support squad can help with the process of intentional inoculation. Touching base with your support system, the people who know you and your strength, about how to deal with difficulties can help counterbalance the haters, doubters, and naysayers who don't know you. By using the affirming voices around you to drive your success, it becomes easier to fight the voices on the outside that try to hinder your path to success.

As you learn to deal with the negativity on the outside, an even more powerful adversary - the mental saboteur - may act as an internal source of conflict. Mitigating this opponent will be discussed in the next chapter as we start to saddle ourselves with our own doubts. Stay tuned!

---

4 Dweck, C. S. (2007). Mindset: The New Psychology of Success. Ballantine Books.

We are all here for similar reasons.

Keep focused.

You will struggle.

And if while you struggle you think most people seem unfazed by the pressure on the surface, know that we are all challenged in unique ways.

Self-awareness is incredibly important if we are to become the best physicians we can be.

Be honest with yourself and keep persevering.

Do no harm.

- Rotsen Rocha

Medical Student

Know that you have value, and that your value is intrinsic to you being a human. Medical school is a relentless process of quantifying and categorizing the human experience. There will be explicit and implicit messages where you will feel that you are not meeting someone else's mark. That is ok; you are here to learn. Evaluation is a dialectical exercise that is as much a reflection of the allegedly dispassionate evaluator as it is on the student. It was challenging for me to realize I was in this sort of system and I found it painful to receive low marks and cruel comments. You should be respectful and professional and learn from everyone, but that does not mean you need to copy or emulate what everyone does. You can learn to NOT be like the person who is evaluating you.

But there are good people too. Look for the people who bring out the best in you, the people who want to invest in you, and the people who like you for who you are. They will often be the people who invest energy in others; the people who leave thank you notes for the cleaning staff or who rush to pick up the phone so their secretary can take a lunch break. These people will show kindness when nobody else is looking and when there is nothing to be gained. Medicine is a team sport, which means that the best role models are those who bring out the best in their teams.

Your superpower will be the ability to show up every day and work really hard because you want to make other people's lives better. Because ultimately it isn't about our grades, our match, our publications, or our pay: it is about the patients who we are there to help.

At the end of the day, may you fall asleep knowing that you did all that you could for your patients and that you remained true to your belief that you can make the world a better place.

- Andrew Meshnick, MD

CHAPTER 5

Building Community Support:
Don't Go At It Alone

I t's the first day of medical school. You're a bright-eyed, enthusiastic student ready to take the next step toward physicianship. As you walk down the halls, you notice that some individuals harbor cautious looks on their faces among your peers while others have no such expression. You find this strange, but before you have the time to ponder what might be happening, you fall. But not onto the floor.

You look around you, and all you notice is darkness, and your senses are disoriented. You don't know how to escape this dreadful pit. But worst of all, you don't even know that this was all preventable. You came into medical school enthusiastic but unprepared. Unlike those who were cautious, you lacked a critical safety net.

Unfortunately, this scenario is all too common in the medical field. For those of you who have gone through medical school and were fortunate enough to avoid this, it is almost certain that you know someone who wasn't as prepared as you. And for those of you who have not yet started medical school, we hope to impart some wisdom about why building a safety net is crucial to not only surviving medical school but thriving in it!

In our role as advisors, we often encounter two types of newly admitted students.

1. High-achieving students who are very familiar with success, had mentors that supported them, a strong family support system, and/or no concerns about housing, finance, or food. For these students, the entire concept of a safety net can be foreign.

2. The journey has been different for the second type of student; it's most likely been full of sweat and grit, ups and downs, challenges, and resilience. Many times, these students have only known success as a fleeting entity.

Dealing with each type of student necessitates a different approach. For the first group, many of whom continuously experienced success, safety, and security and have thus had to think little about fortifying this safety, the approach is relatively straightforward. If you are in this first group, be aware of your position; safety is not always guaranteed. Safety is something that needs to be considered, nurtured, protected, and fought for. Be aware of the resources available to you while becoming a vigilant protector of your safety. That is not to say that there are no other guardians who aim to ensure your safety such as advisors, mentors, and peers. However, YOU must be the primary champion for your safety to be your best self.

For the second group, the approach is more involved since they have known vulnerability for reasons such as unreliable access to mentorship, financial challenges, and housing or food security issues.

And yet, they pushed anyway; they strung together resources and people along the way and made it despite all the challenges. If you are this type of student, the best approach is to consult with your institution to see what resources they can provide you that you may be lacking at this moment.

This may be mentors, financial reassurance, food security, counseling, and/or housing. Establishing a safety net in collaboration with your institution can help foster resilience and appropriate wellness balance, especially given that the medical school environment is very demanding with callous regard for personal challenges.

Whether you're more like the first type or the second, it is the job of advisors, mentors, counselors, and your institution to ensure that you have the proper access to resources and education to secure your safety.

Your safety is breached if you don't have these personal and professional resources to thrive in an environment, whether that be through peer, mentor, financial, housing, and/or health networks. You are vulnerable and feel like things are coming apart. In this case, immediately go to any leader in your environment and say, "I need help!"

However, you must note that rebuilding or fortifying a weakened safety net can be a long and arduous process. But remember that this is not a solo process and that you will have at your back the institution, counselors, mentors, peers, and last but certainly not least, us advisors.

We are here to remind you of your strengths and assets. We are here to remind you not to snowball and take every bad situation as a sign of continual failure. We are here to remind you to be mindful of making decisions when you haven't eaten or when you're super tired. We are here to remind you that medicine is just one aspect of your identity: it's not everything. We are here to remind you to ground yourself in your hobbies, in your passions, your values, or your family. We are here to remind you to remember who you are as a person and to not lose your intersectional identities in your studies. We are really just here to remind you of your humanity.

Just like you should be vigilant about your safety while traveling, you should also be thinking about your safety nets within your learning environment. For instance, if you do not feel safe while traveling in a new country, you won't go out and experience a new cuisine or a different culture.

A similar concept applies to education. If you, as a medical student, do not feel safe and feel like you lack the professional and personal resources to thrive, you may not be able to become your best version.

Work to become more aware of frailties in your safety net and collaborate with your advisors, counselors, peers, and faculty to help protect against insidious breaches of your safety. And if all of this is successful, the once reactive student will be more proactive as they look out for pitfalls.

Six months into my freshman year of undergraduate school I was told by an advisor I needed to change my dream of going to medical school to pursue a more realistic goal.

It felt like being hit by a brick. I'll never forget the words of wisdom given by my mother,

"The doctors I know were not necessarily the top of their class but had the dedication and persistence that allowed them to achieve their dreams."

Following this advice, I stopped thinking about the amount of time the medical school acceptance process was taking me (an additional 6 years) and continued to tell myself that time passes regardless of if I am working towards a goal.

I decided that I would persevere and continue doing all that I could to make myself a competitive applicant regardless of my challenges and obstacles.

- Summer McCloud

Medical Student

CHAPTER 6

When Dreams Become Reality:
Time to Get Down!

Can we catch our dreams? Many of us continually chase them every day in hopes of grasping that which we yearn for. But the most important aspect of a dream is often overlooked. It is not capturing the dream that is most pertinent but the growth mindset that we adopt while pursuing the dream. What is embedded at the core of our dreams is an aspirational element regarding our ability to dream to evolve for the better. A dreamer must not simply chase the dream, but always envision the possibilities and probabilities to be accomplished along the journey.

For a true dreamer, achieving your dream is somewhat elusive. If medicine is your dream, you can become a doctor. But if you are a true dreamer, being a doctor is not the limit. Once you become a physician, the dream evolves as you continue to chase excellence in the field of medicine, which, by its very nature, is constantly advancing towards greater heights of servant leadership.

As you commit to pursuing your dream of helping others, resilience is a critical aspect necessary to overcome inevitable and unexpected obstacles you will encounter. The first inevitable obstacle is doubt. Can you accomplish your dream of becoming a physician who continually strives for excellence and improvement despite the journey being incredibly tough? Doubt will always be there, whether it is at the beginning of your journey or the middle of your journey. You may doubt your ability to become a physician, and even when you are a physician, you may doubt the extent to which you are actually making a difference.

The second inevitable obstacle that you will encounter is a feeling of helplessness because you cannot always change the outcome of an unfortunate health condition. Despite your best efforts, death may be inevitable during the course of the patient's diagnosis.

Relying on your peer network is essential for combating these inevitable feelings of doubt or helplessness. Because of the conservative nature of the medical field, feelings of doubt and helplessness may feel unexpected when, in reality, they are normal. Part of building your resilience and navigating these inevitable obstacles is understanding how to build an appropriate support system wherein you feel comfortable sharing these feelings and learning from others who have been through this process. In addition to building personal alliances, looking at the successes you have built while analyzing how your peers have navigated these challenges can help minimize these overwhelming feelings.

In addition to the inevitable obstacles, you may encounter certain unexpected ones. The first unexpected obstacle may be fear. This could be fear about your inability to accomplish your task of being a doctor or it could be anxiety-driven thoughts about accidentally hurting someone.

The second unexpected obstacle may be a change in how you view your role in the medical field. For example, you may have wanted to help people through surgery for years, but then you suddenly find out that you actually do not like surgery during your clinical years.

Although these feelings may spark some fear, a critical step in the journey to physicianship is taking a step back and recognizing that there is no set path. Part of the call to medicine is figuring out where you fit in.

Sometimes, you lose your way. You let challenges get to you and think you are not on the right path. You lost sight of your 'Why' and no longer have any intrinsic motivation. And this feeling can prove to be a major hurdle.

Your intrinsic motivation is the anchor of your resilience. If this anchor is not there, then you have nothing. If we view ourselves as having a "tank" of resilience – and your intrinsic motivation is gone – then not only is this tank empty, but it is actually completely missing. However, this is not the end of the line, as many people have experienced a loss of resiliency at some point during their lives regardless of occupation, age, gender, skill, or any other metric you can think of.

In this case, we need to work on getting our tank back and filling it up to prevent this loss again. For many, the best way of achieving the former is by circling back to their 'Why.' Remind yourself of your entire journey up to this point; you started this path for a reason. Think of who you are trying to serve. Did you go into medicine to improve your community? To address an injustice you have seen impacting your loved ones? Regardless of exactly what it is, you need to remind yourself of why you chose to go into medicine.

Filling up your tank of resiliency is something that can be done at any time. The earlier, the better. But, now and again, you may face some dire setbacks and have to work from the ground up. In either case, there are a multitude of ways you can go about filling up your tank. One major way is by reaching out to your support network, whether it be your peers, mentors, advisors, counselors, etc. By letting them know whenever you are going through a life challenge, you will be able to share the mental burden of whatever it is that is weighing down upon you. Moreover, you can also use them as models or inspiration. They each have their own stories with their own challenges.

And yet, they persevered in their individual endeavors and most likely have advice on what they have done to improve their resilience. Thus, you can use their advice as a template for how you want to conduct your own journey.

Another method is to envision your ideal self from how you dress to how you want to interact with future colleagues, patients, family, and friends. Use this as a tool, as a motivator of why you are doing what you are doing. By envisioning the future that you want, you may feel more motivated along the path you need to take, especially if you use tangible methods like vision boards rather than just abstract ideas.

To walk the path of physicianship, you should ideally be one who pursues your dreams with dogged determination and maximum flexibility. You should strive to be a continual dreamer who is open to evolution but still fixed on your core goal. While you may not change intrinsically, your dreams may evolve as you get more familiar with the environment and get more experience under your belt.

Strive to be a forever dreamer.

The task at hand may appear daunting, but do it anyway. Your resilience can take you farther than you ever thought possible.

If, at first, you find it difficult to keep pushing forward, take a step back and recognize how far you have come. All of your triumphs and tribulations have lead you to this exact moment.

Don't stop now. Wake up and choose resilience.

- Berline Francis, MD

You can feel frustrated, break down in tears, and question if these sacrifices are worth it. What you cannot do is give up. Remember you are not just giving up on yourself, but you are also giving up on those who believe in your greatness even when you do not.

- Brittney Rodriguez, MD

We find strength through our most difficult struggles.

Surround yourself with those who lift you up, challenge you, and can make you laugh through those times of darkness.

Visualize yourself accomplishing each of your goals. You are brave, you are courageous, and you will continue your path toward success!

- Kiersten Sydnor

GEMS Alumnus

SECTION 3:

Challenges

In an inspiring TED talk called "Get comfortable with being uncomfortable," Luvvie Ajayi Jones compares challenges to her experience skydiving. She states that sitting on the edge of a plane when waiting to jump off represents your comfort zone, but jumping out of the plane represents you preventing fear from dictating your actions and taking control of your own destiny.[5]

The next few chapters are exactly about this sensation – facing your internal obstacles, such as imposter syndrome, that might force you to stay in your comfort zone, yet defeating these feelings and achieving your dreams by taking a leap of self-confidence.

---

[5] YouTube. (2018). Get comfortable with being uncomfortable. YouTube. Retrieved September 16, 2023, from https://www.youtube.com/watch?v=QijH4UAqGD8.

SECTION 3 OPENING:

Magdalena's Poem

"If You Struggle Long Enough"

This is the year I survive to live
no vivir para sobrevivir.
Perfectionism isn't circular
no seré una impostora en mi propia piel.
Feelings of inadequacy will be vanished away
no tomarán control de mi vida.

This is the year the imposter's mind doesn't conquer
ya no dudaré de mí misma.
The labels can't penetrate my essence
ya no marcaré las casillas.
My voices will be heard
ya no pisaran a mi raza en mi presencia.
I am who I am; not a fraud

This is the year the mask fades as the seed emerges
tomaré el toro por los cuernos.
My loss will no longer weigh me down
luchará contra la soledad.
This is the year we stand united as outliers
mi benda se cayo.
Los llantos del pueblo mexicatl y de los niños en las jaulas se escucharan

This is the year the oppressor is conquered
el sistema que miente, mata,maltrata, manipula.
This is the year the rejected reign
sobrevivir para vivir.
This is the year our struggles empower

Viviré una vida through which
Mis luchas florecen
My trust in el proceso will be legendary, game-changing;
Este es el año

- Magdalena Macias, Pre-Medical Student

CHAPTER 7

Part I

Squash the Saboteurs Inside:
Conditioning Mental Stamina

As a child, you may have played games that require the skill of deception. In games like mafia, you had to conceal your true identity in order to prevent your fellow players from catching on to your role as an outsider. In a professional setting, you may feel like you are playing a similar "game," except it is not as voluntary and not nearly as fun - *the game of Imposter Syndrome.*

Although you have all the attributes and skill sets necessary to carry out a particular position effectively and appropriately, imposter syndrome affects your perception, making you feel like you don't belong amongst your peers. Multiple things can trigger this.

First, other people within your professional setting may have advanced expertise with respect to the role you were navigating, causing you to feel like a beginner. Or, other people within your professional setting may question your credentials through circuitous actions such as asking you to justify your qualifications when no one else has been asked to do so.

As you start to feel that others are more qualified than you to get the job done, you ask "Am I even supposed to be here?"

Imposter syndrome is relevant for all but is of particular importance amongst those from underrepresented backgrounds who are already more likely to experience marginalization, often in the form of subtle microaggressions. One such example comes from Dave's time at a boot camp for health profession educators. He was recruited as 1 of 40 people to participate in a week-long professional development opportunity. The selection process included an intense international application from which the cream of the crop were selected by experts in the field. Once he arrived at the workshop and looked at everyone's CVs, Dave started to question if he belonged, especially as one of the few people of color there.

As he read through his peers' CVs, the list of higher degrees of M.D, Ph.D., MPH, & MBA went on and on when he didn't even have his Master's degree at that point.

Despite the discrepancy in credentials, he still held on to his resolve as he knew he was there because the selection committee and his mentors recognized his skill level and potential to grow.

The boot camp included various journal clubs where participants discussed articles. One of the clubs discussed an imposter syndrome article, during which someone smirkingly sniped, "Hey Dave, you might be especially interested in this article."

At this point, multiple feelings ran across his mind:

1) This person thinks they are intimidating me
2) Maybe I am an imposter?
3) I am a resilient fighter who does belong!

As these voices battled for dominance in his head, the second, more doubtful voice began to take over. However, something happened soon after to change this feeling.

The journal club also featured case study presentations in front of everyone in an amphitheater-style room, typically accompanied by the attendees' shouts of detailed citations like "Journal of American Medicine, February 2008!"; to say the least, this level of expertise was intimidating. When the facilitators asked him to present a summary of the case study at hand, Dave nervously entered the pit of the amphitheater where he faced his peers who eagerly awaited to spectate his performance. Standing inside the pit, he thought his secret might be exposed. The secret that he may not truly belong among his peers, but soon he flipped his mindset. He recognized that at the time of the presentation, he was the presenter and thus, the expert. He then continued making his case as if he were prosecuting in a legal courtroom. Strong arguments, supported by powerful oration.

With this mindset, he could engage with people who may have known more than he did with a level of sturdy confidence. Towards the end of the presentation, people applauded and even the facilitator complimented him on his performance. After this, he felt affirmed. The compliments on a job well done continued as the days went on, and he recognized that the people who came up to him were authentic.

He recognized that he did indeed belong there and those who purposefully made doubtful comments didn't matter to his professional development.

Ultimately, although we all have momentary pauses, individuals from historically underrepresented backgrounds who have had to fight to demonstrate competencies throughout their lives can continually experience imposter syndrome at every new level of success. They may feel that they must consistently demonstrate that they belong because of limiting societal perspectives on what those of minority identities can and should do.

This type of imposter syndrome facing minority individuals isn't transient and is far more insidious, always lurking beneath the surface due to the endless barrage of microaggressions, biases, and other triggers one faces within society. Once this continuous imposter syndrome makes you feel isolated, it continues to prey upon this feeling and emboldens the mental saboteur to amplify the doubts that you may be feeling. This mental saboteur, a manifestation of your own discouraging thoughts, knows you best. It knows your strengths and inner weaknesses and, most importantly, how to psychologically work through your defense mechanisms.

Creating a reservoir of instances in which you have successfully demonstrated your expertise along your professional journey, like Dave's personal example above, can be a useful antidote to fight the mental saboteur. Navigating this challenge requires being affirmed by this reservoir and pulling from it when faced with doubts to condition your mental stamina.

Building up this defense barrier takes time and effort. If you are still in the process of assembling your defenses, the saboteur could peek through the top of the barrier. However, continually fortifying your reservoir through affirmations, self-reflection, and personal experiences can help you shut out the mental saboteur with a highly engaged responsive attitude that facilitates greater levels of resilience.

Fighting back against the voice of the imposter also requires authentic affirmations. Surround yourself with people who give you affirmations based on your successes to date. We often don't recognize life's successes – whether we were a concert violinist, graduating athlete, etc. If you don't have people nearby who can you give you these affirmations, go searching for inspirational quotes online or pick up inspirational greeting cards at a store that you can see, read, and put up around your study space or office. You can do this!

When moments of overwhelming feelings of unbelonging come up, keep composure in the moment and go to a quiet place to decompress. Talk to a mentor and get reaffirmed. Constantly acknowledging your successes with the help of affirming mentors can help you build up the critical resilience needed to fight back against triggers of imposter syndrome.

You belong here.

You worked yourself to the bone and defeated all odds to get here.

You are your family's American dream and it is your turn to fight for all the immigrant families who do not have a voice.

Girls who doubt themselves look up to you.

You can be a role model for them but you have to start believing in yourself first.

- Pei-Ying Kobres, MD

The important question is not,

"*Am I smart enough?*";

rather,

"*Am I prepared enough?*"

- Francis Navarra, MD

Part 2

Squash the Saboteurs Inside:
Conditioning Mental Stamina

In 2015, as Susan sat in her job interview for Senior Associate Dean for Diversity, Equity, and Inclusion at Georgetown University School of Medicine, she felt a wave of intimidation wash over her.

A few days earlier, she started practicing for her interviews and expressed her nervousness to her mentors and colleagues. Although she had a doctorate in education leadership, expertise, and experience, as a non-MD she knew she would be in a room full of physicians, medical experts in their fields, and she felt like she didn't belong. Questions like "Do I know what I would talk about to these experts who have been working for such a long time at this university?" started running through her head. As she felt the jitters before her interview began, the words of one of her mentors grounded her. The mentor simply pointed out that the doctors who may interview her aren't experts in the topics that she was an expert in such as diversity, equity, inclusion, belonging, and culture building.

In other words, everyone has their own areas of expertise, accompanied by areas of limited knowledge, even professions that hold prestigious statuses in society such as physicians or deans.

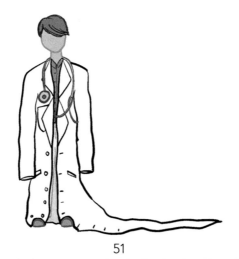

More specifically, doctors often have much to learn about cultural humility and competency around diversity, equity, and inclusion. Medicine, despite its critical role in society, is still a field plagued by challenges in structural racism, bias, classism, etc., all issues that Susan's outsider expertise could start to mitigate and address. That being said, using your past skill sets and experiences as a source of confidence to thwart imposter syndrome doesn't mean you ignore humility. No matter the status of one's environment, there is still much to be learned.

This example speaks to another quality of imposter syndrome in addition to those explored within Part 1. Imposter syndrome is caused by doubts that are reflections of one's learning and working environment. For instance, in Susan's experience, her imposter syndrome arose from initial microaggressions regarding things like. "You look too young to be a dean. Are you a student here?" These comments are designed by the environment to detract from your impact and distract from what you can contribute with your unique opinion.

Lately, there has been a shift in the conversation from the individual to the whole. In the past, discussions surrounding imposter syndrome have focused on individual pathologies.

Honing in on questions like:

"What is wrong with you that you feel this way?" or

"Are you good enough to be in this professional setting?"

However, this framing is unhelpful and misleading.

The focus must shift from individual pathologies to the faults within one's environment that foster hostile ideas telling people that they don't belong. That is to say, imposter syndrome is less of an indicator of personal failing or moral ineptitude that you aren't cut out, but a reflection of the learning and working environments. Structural inequities, microaggressions, and other instances of implicit and explicit bias that are pervasive in professional environments can cause one to feel gaslit and reinforce feelings of alienation within an organization or learning environment.

How can we combat this phenomenon and cultivate an environment that is an affirmer of growth instead of an enabler of impostership? First off, affirmations that salute successes and uplift individuals whilst acknowledging the role of restrictive environments can help turn the narrative on its head.

By saying and writing affirmations, you can become what you envision. These daily affirming habits can build the stamina to tap into the reservoir that you need to withstand attacks on you from the environment.

Another critical part of combatting imposter syndrome from an environmental point of view is cultivating peer-to-peer support networks. For instance, Susan and Dave championed the Build and Belong initiative, wherein medical student peers shared their fears, successes, and experiences with each other. Not only does this mitigate imposter syndrome by decreasing feelings of social isolation, but it also creates a sense of hope to succeed. Creating a group identity that embraces doubts while navigating your medical journey through interventions like these can normalize discussions regarding isolation and take away the source from which imposter syndrome springs from.

Our book is a personification of this initiative.

Each affirmation contributes to the peer network through examples of shared experiences and the growth that resulted from them.

One student's resilience and stories of recovering from missteps being shared with another student can help fill up the resiliency reservoir of the latter student as they learn to defeat the feeling of being an imposter on their path of professional identity formation.

Ultimately, to fulfill the promises of a culture of teamwork and cooperative learning within medicine, engaging learners through structural support systems within the learning environment that ensure equitable reinforcement can help cultivate a nurturing culture of affirmation.

What is for you will always be for you. No matter how you shake it up, or run away, the path that is destined for you has already been laid before you. It is those little moments that pull at your heart and get your mind thinking of the "what if's."

What if I stopped sleeping on myself? What if I was as encouraging to myself as I am to others? What if I got a little uncomfortable? What if I went all out for myself? Often times we are embedding ourselves into spaces and places that are not designed for us. However sunshine, these places need YOU.

The younger generation needs you to be brave and step out of your head of insecurities. They need this because someone unknowingly did just this for you. Are you going to let your self deprecating thoughts leave the path unclear for the next person that looks like you? This does not mean easy, it only means attainable with the correct dedication, passion, tenacity and leadership. So show up for yourself daily and go forth, bravely!

- Jasmine Rice

Medical Student

Word of advice, stop doubting your abilities!

You are capable and able to succeed.

You made it to this point, right, despite all odds?

The moment you let those feelings of inadequacy creep up,
your anxiety wins.

Do not let your mistakes stop you from getting up and trying again.

Let the lessons you've learned along the way guide you.

Remember you are your hardest critic.

- Adedamola Badewa, MD

CHAPTER 8

Wins:
Small and Big Ones Along Your Journey

As students walk the halls of Georgetown University School of Medicine, they now see portraits of influential women. We even have a campaign around this called "Women on the Walls" (WOW), which features powerful figures and mentors like Dean Joy Williams, who played a pivotal role in the professional development of more than four hundred doctors from underrepresented backgrounds. These portraits represent the medical school environment, affirming students by visually representing symbolic successes that are possible for everyone. However, despite the cultural shifts that encourage environments to be more inclusive in affirming all, environments continue to forgo affirming those who are marginalized.

In this instance, it is important to affirm yourself and internally validate your successes, even if you are not seeing external validation. These successes can be of any size - not just the big milestones like landing an NIH grant or a faculty position at a large research institute. It also recognizes the small, incremental wins that one day build up the stamina necessary to achieve *transformational* successes.

Now, some may view acknowledging success as being boastful. But, during your professional development in medicine, acknowledging success is not a prideful act meant to boost the infamous "god complex" that many associate with physicianship. Instead, it is a necessary act that fills your tank with resilience to motivate you to take on or push through challenging times. Whether you fill this tank before coming to medical school or build your resilience tank after coming to medical school in intentional ways, such as by journaling your successes or sharing them with trusted peers and/or affirming mentors, filling your resiliency reservoir by sharing your personal successes is critical for self-preservation. It is critical to keep you in the game despite frustrating inevitable challenges or the high emotional, mental, and physical toll associated with the sacrifices that are ubiquitous throughout medicine.

In addition to filling up your resiliency reservoir, validating your successes is also critical for showing your appreciation for all of those who helped you along the way and for inspiring those around you. For instance, Susan is honest and open about validating her successes and the invisible toil behind these successes. Successes like learning to balance being a mom and a dean in higher education or being promoted from Assistant Professor to Associate Professor are not just hers as her leadership role makes it so that her successes are felt and seen by those around her.

Another reason for celebrating your successes in this field is that medicine can be a land filled with turmoil. With physician burnout rates rapidly rising, shifting the paradigm to positively nurture the careers of future doctors by encouraging early reflection of one's growth and resiliency can hopefully counter some of the toxic aspects associated with this field. Especially in times of the pandemic, this paradigm shift has become abundantly clear.

During the pandemic, we often saw viral videos of health professionals lining at the doors of recently recovered COVID patients in the ICU, clapping and cheering for joy, as they not only celebrate their patient's discharge but also all of the personal sacrifices that went into providing care. In this way, longitudinally and intentionally reflecting on your own successes and affirming yourself to build your own trophy case is a way to grow the resiliency necessary to positively and openly embrace the physicianship journey.

Medicine is demanding and requires great sacrifice.

Celebrating the smiles of your patients, and the words of special appreciation from their families will sustain your calling to serve in medicine.

- Mfoniso Okon, MD

Success is often defined for us rather than defined by us.

A 70% cutoff, a "P" next to the course name on your transcript or a "well done" from someone higher up on the metaphorical totem pole. The first two more objective, the latter subjective.

Either way, we are used to being told we are on the right path and if we deviate, we are given feedback to correct our trajectory along the way.

The more objective forms of success were and still are moments to celebrate, be it going out with friends on a night on the town or simply visiting family back home. The important thing is this: celebrate what you have accomplished, no matter how small.

The first few years it may be those required exams that are your motive for celebration and that is great!

As you progress and the number of written exams decreases, you still need to find ways to celebrate the other forms of successes you experience.

This was a realization I came to when I found myself not going out as often or simply having fun anymore.

Burnout is real, but so are the people around to help you when it does happen. Go out for a drink, go to that dinner, visit grandma, watch that movie or find someone to watch it with you. You will always have a reason to celebrate, because you chose (in my opinion) the most humbling profession to practice. That itself, deserves a toast.

- Jason Chavez, MD

Identity

To be a physician requires a transformation of the individual—one does not simply learn to be a physician, one becomes a physician.

— Abraham Fuks and colleagues, "The Foundation of Physicianship"

Inspired by the above quote, the following chapters explore your personal and professional identity.

Becoming a physician involves a key transformation as you embrace your personal identity and interweave it with your professional identity that forms on the journey to physicianship.

As you will appreciate when reading the following chapters, embracing these identities are critical to becoming the playwright of your own dreams and creating a sustainable, wellness filled journey to physicianship.

SECTION 4 OPENING:

Mariama's Poem

"My Black Affirmation"

Black is Aspiring & Achieving
Black is Anticipating Adversity
Black is an Art Form
Black is Bold
Black is Beautiful
Black is Beating the Odds
Black is Building, Believing, & Becoming
Black is Counting Coins & Blessings
Black is Culture & Community
Black is Climbing a Ladder
Black is Can't Stop, Won't Stop
Black is Deep & Deep Rooted
Black is Deliberate Destination
Black is Discipline & Determination
Black is Dancing to that Beat Called Life
Black is Daring & Dreaming
Black is Extraordinary Excellence
Black is Expression & Creativity
Black is Family & Faith First
Black is Forgiving
Black is Flexing & Finessing
Black is Glinting Golden in the Sun
Black is Gratitude & Grace
Black is Hard Work
Black is Hip Hop, Afrobeats, R&B, Reggae, & Jazz
Black is Illustrious
Black is Innovation & Intellect

Black is Joyful
Black is Jammin' & Just Kidding
Black is Just One Drop
Black is Kinks & Locs
Black is Keepin' it Real
Black is Loud, Louder than Life
Black is Liberation
Black is Lived Experiences
Black is Learning & Growing
Black is a Mix of Every Shade
Black is Mother Africa
Black is Malcolm X & MLK
Black is Next Level
Black is No Justice, No Peace
Black is Overcoming
Black is One Love
Black is Open Heart, Mind, & Spirit
Black is Perseverance & Progress
Black is Power Reclaimed
Black is Proud
Black is Queens & Kings
Black is Righteous
Black is Resilience Deserving of Respect
Black is Soulful & Strong
Black is Smart - Street Smart, Life Smart, & Book Smart
Black Stands OUT
Black is Spoken Word
Black is Suffering & Smiling
Black is Sacrifice
Black is Success Despite Adversity
Black is Tenacity
Black is Trailblazing
Black is Uniting & Uplifting

Black is Unbelievably Unbreakable
Black is Values & Virtue
Black is Wisdom
Black is Welcoming & Warm
Black is Working Twice as Hard to get Half as Much
Black is Wildin'
Black is Where There's a Will, There's a Way
Black is X-tra
Black is Yelling YOLO
Black is Yes We Can & Yes We Will
Black is Zest & Zeal
Yet somehow, Black feels like a shadow I live under
The world has gone out of its way to obscure my Blackness
To convince me that my Blackness is a shadow I've been casted under
I am casted under
Because the world chooses not to see Black as clearly as I do
Why has the world chosen not to see Black as clearly as I do?
I just can't understand
Why being Black, my greatest honor
Could be the source of any pain
This is undoubtedly the world's greatest shame
But the reality is...
Black is the fuel to my FIRE
My Blackness, Our Blackness
Is our brightness, gifted by God!
Why should my Blackness illicit your darkness?
Because you choose to be blind?
Open your eyes & see
Our Blackness gifted to us by Almighty Allah
Shines bright! It has and will
Illuminate the world

- Mariama Jallow-Olanrewaju, MD

CHAPTER 9

Physician:
Know Thyself

I t is safe to say that many families have a pre-written "playbook" for the younger generation. While not actually written, this playbook is still very much real and is meant to encode behaviors and dictate various decisions to ensure success. Cultural and identity-related factors culminate into this instructive manual as all the hopes of *abuelos, moms, pops, aunties and uncles* ride on the shoulders of the manuscript's protagonist who is viewed as the generational champion of the family. However, while the writers of this playbook view this as protective guidance, those expected to follow this predetermined path have a different perspective as they are pressured to obey crowds of voices over their own.

Due to the collective nature of this playbook, the pressure felt by those expected to follow it comes in many different forms. Not only is pressure created due to overly ambitious goals set by family, but it can also be created by dissuasive identity-based beliefs that make up the playbook. For instance, some family members discourage pursuing medicine in favor of learning a trade skill that runs in the family despite the fact that the individual themselves may value medicine over the trade skill. Furthermore, culturally dependent beliefs can also create pressure. An example of this may be when familial figures from patriarchal cultures discourage women from pursuing their passions.

Although these sets of cookie-cutter familial expectations based on identity or culture can sometimes come from well-meaning intentions, students have to contend with the resulting pressure as they become constrained within the bounds of the pages of this pre-programmed playbook.

The most essential step to combating these pressures is to unlearn the playbook. Instead of limiting yourself to following what others have told you to do, create your own manuscript in your own voice – improvise your own way through the play! A key principle towards achieving this is discernment. Discernment represents the process of stepping away from the expectations that others have of you and instead stepping towards your own internalized agenda regarding the path that you deem is an appropriate reflection of your passions. In other words, it represents *knowing thyself.*

Discernment allows you to create space for yourself, to reinvent and discover new aspects of your identity while you move away from the chatter surrounding familial or community expectations. Through this process, you can break away from the cocoon of the pre-written playbook authored by families/mentors/others to materialize your sense of comfort while mastering an openness towards learning and growth. As you push through the crowd of watchful eyes, past the voices of expectations, and over your own preconceived notions influenced by these expectations of what you should be, you begin to journey towards knowing yourself as you find the key to carving your own path to success.

Why are discernment and the process of canceling out the noise of preconceived expectations critical? Because it is fundamental to realizing your intrinsic motivation. One's intrinsic motivation in medicine can be encapsulated by a few basic questions: What makes you want to pursue medicine? Is it the desire to help others, be a respected professional, be financially or personally secure, or other factors? Simply put, what personally drives you towards medicine regardless of what external entities may have said about your fit for physicianship?

Especially in a critical service-oriented profession like medicine, if you aren't taking moments to quiet everything around you - all the voices of mentors, family members, and role models that occupy your mental space – it becomes particularly difficult to self-reflect and say, "Why do I really want to pursue medicine?"

Without taking moments to remind yourself of why you are pursuing this field or if your reasons for pursuing medicine aren't enough to keep you driven, intrinsic motivation can be hard to decipher. Discerning your own space and using this introspection to establish your personal intrinsic motivational force can help you throughout the medical journey and build resilience as you become stronger academically and mentally. In other words, knowing yourself and finding your intrinsic motivation is critical to dealing with challenges down the road since motivation acts as an anchor in the face of inevitable turbulent challenges that arise during your journey to becoming a physician.

At this point you may be asking what all this has to do with affirmations? As you piece out your authentic series of reasons that drive you towards medicine, affirmations provide an intentional opportunity to build on this anchor of intrinsic motivation as they help bolster it in times of rough turbulence. Even in the face of dissuading attitudes from cultural, community, or familial figures, affirmations can help you silence the crowd and bolster your personal drive.

At times, supportive encouragement that holds you accountable from affirming figures can be just what the doctor ordered to grow your resilience. Reading an affirmation, internalizing it, personalizing it, and applying it to realizing your own dreams in the face of crushing pressures brought on by external expectations or failures is essential. Strategically reaching out to others that validate you, encourage you, and remind you of the direction that you need to take in the process of *knowing thyself* can help you silence the overstimulating noises around you. As you know thyself, you can mitigate dissuasive beliefs encoded within your community's playbook, allowing you to better incorporate positive affirmations that help push you along your goal to becoming your own playwright.

All things that are worth it and sustainable in

life take time, so when that journey feels long

and treacherous,

remember you are preparing for a career of a lifetime.

- Marsiyana Henricus, MD

CHAPTER 10

Take Your Vitamins:
Nourishing Your Journey for Life

Doctor's orders!

Fill your medical school medicine cabinet with these essential vitaminal values:

Vitamin A for "assurance" that the path you have started is one that you can finish since you have seen evidence of your growth points. Finding a bottle of Vitamin A is not as easy as going to the supplement section of a store. In other words, although many tend to look for assurance external to them, it must be found internally. Be humble and assured that you can continue on this journey due to your past and present successes.

Vitamin B stands for "be the best." Let us put it this way - recognize that you have the gifts and talents necessary to be the best version of yourself. Continually improve yourself to be your finest version, armed with the confidence generated by the resiliency spawned from the successes of your journey.

Vitamin C for "consistency." Partnered with the assurance that you can achieve goals on your path and your desire to project the best version of yourself, consistency in the medical school journey is an easily achievable goal.

Taking Vitamins A, B, and C helps you develop the conviction to take Vitamin D for "diligence." Being intentionally diligent on your journey and executing your goals is not just a critical component of success for yourself, but also one that allows you to be a supportive model for others.

Now we have Vitamin E, which stands for "excellence." As you accomplish your goals of extracting and maintaining the aforementioned vitaminal values, you demonstrate excellence - something we all aspire to achieve. However, excellence must be anchored in humility, a critical component of physicianship.

Medicine necessitates that you model excellence for yourself and your peers to inspire one another, but this must be done in a selfless manner as a humble leader should espouse the values of servant leadership. Although excellence can be elusive, taking your Vitamin E and being in the correct mindset can ensure that you are always working towards it.

Finally, we have Vitamin K, the most important vitamin. "Keepsakes of mindfulness" are important because they give you a chance to take stock of what is happening around you, your intentions, and the things you appreciate. These keepsakes of mindfulness can take on various forms of self-care, whether that be daily reflective journaling to clear out the cobwebs in your mind, meditation, engaging in conversations with peers who are non-judgemental listeners, or faith traditions. Some personal examples include things like exercising or creating a vision board to maintain her determination for Susan or for Dave, watching Perry Mason while having a conversation with a member of his supportive peer network like his friend of 35 years, Colin, who pushes his horizons and provides feedback in a healthy way.

These check-in activities ensure that you are being mindful of refueling your vitamins while reflecting on areas that may need an extra boost. They can encourage you to ask foundational questions like "Who am I today?" "Is this still the right path for me?" "Am I still finding joy in what I am doing or studying?"

For instance, after this period of self-reflection, you may feel unsettled and realize that you haven't been the best version of yourself. In other words, you haven't been taking your Vitamin B. From this point on, you can plan to complete the necessary actions to support your Vitamin B intake as you brainstorm ideas to always give the best version of yourself by growing in innovative ways.

These six vitaminal values are essential for nourishing your desire to be successful, helping you to consciously foster habits in your professional identity that will carry your life's lessons to the future and support you as you thrive in your journey.

Since medicine is a field riddled with physician burnout, taking your vitamins early on, knowing how to nourish yourself at different points, and intentionally taking stock of yourself at least once a week, can routinely maintain a healthy wellness lifestyle in medicine. This allows you to be a better physician with a pool of resilience that acts as a focal point for your own wellness that then allows you to care for others.

With all this being said, it is paramount that you take your own vitamins! Don't take other people's vitamins because what they need might not be what you need. Give yourself the time to figure out your own timeline and affirmational needs.

Finally, be sure to celebrate the joys and victories of your peers. Authentically acknowledging your peers can augment your vitaminal values and act as a healthy way to cope with the competitiveness of the medical field. Genuinely rejoicing in the success of others while also taking care of yourself by addressing your vitaminal needs can foster growth and build the humility necessary to blossom into an exceptional servant leader.

The journey that you are undertaking is long and lonely at times. Quitting may seem to be an attractive option at some points. I encourage you to keep your mission at the forefront to keep you pushing forward when you are in these moments. As a Christian believer, I firmly profess that God's graces upon us are given for the sake of blessing others. With this in mind, I want you to think of those who will depend on you to be their blessing and let them give you fuel. They are the reason why you are privileged to pursue your calling! Lastly, please be careful with allowing material possessions to motivate you. When the going gets tough, material things may not inspire you since there are many other ways to get those things outside of being a physician. Stay encouraged. God Bless!

- Tyrel Powell

Medical Student

Through the path towards becoming a physician, doubt and feeling the need to quit are unfortunately frequently raised in one's head.

The long study hours, voluminous content, and the sheer number of standardized testing throughout the years, combined with the possibility to be wiped out of the competition with any sort of failure can often shatter your confidence.

I am no stranger to these feelings, but I have been able to find a mechanism that has provided me with the strength and perseverance to push through.

Although sometimes it may feel counterintuitive, given how tightly packed academic schedules can be, taking some time out of your day and dedicating it to your favorite hobby can be that extra boost that relieves the tension. I remember as I was studying for the MCAT the first time, I dedicated all my time and effort towards studying and practicing as many questions as I could. This resulted in my mental health taking a huge hit, and the effects showed in the final score.

The second time, I decided to take a more holistic approach, and ensure that my own mental health is part of the equation as I took on this monster of an exam. I reserved certain parts of my study schedule for my personal hobbies such as photography, chess, and watching some good old English football league.

Even though I spent less time studying the second time, I ended up having a much better score. I have always encouraged people to find a hobby, preferably one that is different from the profession they are seeking, and explore it during stressful times.

- Parsa Mahmoudi

Medical Student

You are **powerful**

You are **strong**

You are **successful**

Be kind to yourself

YOU GOT THIS!

Never underestimate the opportunity to learn from a disappointment in life. Although it may be uncomfortable, we can have our greatest opportunity for growth in moments of discomfort. Think about all of your successes to date that started with a major challenge.

Look at you now!

- David L. Taylor

Senior Dean for Student Learning

On your pathway to success, check-in with yourself regularly to leave space for your own growth, flexibility and change. Our dreams can evolve in ways we never anticipated. Give them space to sprout, flourish and outgrow your own expectations. Protect your dreams from naysayers as well and keep your garden of possibility well-tended to and nurtured with others who provide warmth, encouragement and vision for what you could become.

- Susan M. Cheng

Senior Associate Dean for Diversity, Equity, Inclusion & Belonging

Associate Professor of Family Medicine

Printed in the United States
by Baker & Taylor Publisher Services